PROPHECY & CHANCE

CONTENTS

Scan this code to access
the *Behind the Lines* website
with cartoon GIFs, descriptive
labels and more.

04 Introduction

06 Reinventing the Wheel (of Fortune)

10 2021: A Year of Fury and Fatigue

16 Prophecy & Chance

18 Political Cartoonist of the Year

20 Political Life Lines

38 The Empress

52 A Sporting Chance

64 Roll(out) of the Dice

82 Wheel of Fortune

98 Mars Retrograde

114 Bad Omens

130 Consulting the Oracle

146 About the Artists

INTRODUCTION

Daryl Karp AM
Director, Museum of Australian Democracy

Behind the Lines is an annual institution, MoAD's most popular exhibition, and an ongoing tribute to the important role political cartoonists play in our democracy by calling out naked emperors and holding power to account. Over the years we have watched on as the number of cartoonists employed in traditional media has shrunk. New technologies have enabled an unstoppable tide of disruption and satire, and critique can now find expression in myriad forms and platforms that exist outside the op-ed pages of physical newspapers. Lucien Leon eloquently explores this wave of change in his essay in this catalogue.

Pleasingly, we can see that cartoonists are successfully navigating this shifting landscape. Practitioners have found new ways to connect with audiences. New artists have entered the fray, challenging conventional forms of practice and finding a new generation of devotees. Reflecting this dynamism, *Behind the Lines* likewise continues to evolve. This year, alongside some talented familiar faces, we are introducing several first-time contributors who reflect our diverse democracy.

In last year's *Behind the Lines* (subtitled *2020, A Dog's Breakfast*), Cathy Wilcox, Political Cartoonist of the Year, created one of the most memorable visuals: her 'COVID puppy'. This red-ribboned Bichon Frise injected much-needed humour into the uncertainty and upheaval of what many argued was a 'dog' of a year. And 2021 has proved to be no less challenging. Global issues such as the pandemic and climate change continued to weigh heavily. In Canberra, familiar 'business as usual' headlines — leadership jockeying and funding scandals — were pushed aside by allegations of wrongdoing and a gender-

#HelpAfghanistan

This year's judges, Casey Briggs, Marcus Hughes, Lucien Leon, Nanette Louchart-Fletcher, Mary-Louise McLaws, Steph Tisdell, Holly Williams and myself, named Sydney-based cartoonist Glen Le Lievre as this year's deserving winner. With his pathos-infused GIFs in 2020, he was the first *Behind the Lines* cartoonist to present digital works. This year his work stood out to the judges for his skill at capturing an issue without the need for words.

hostile workplace culture at the heart of our democracy, Parliament House. Cartoonists and audiences alike struggled with a year that felt the same, but worse.

Behind the Lines 2021 draws on a feature of the zeitgeist — the prevalence of predictive models in our daily lives. Be it interest rates, global warming or COVID-19 numbers, 2021 has highlighted how our experience of uncertainty is being balanced, and sometimes fed, by expert advice: the Treasury's *2021 Intergenerational Report*, the Intergovernmental Panel on Climate Change's *AR6 Climate Change 2021* report and the *Doherty Modelling Report for National Cabinet*, to name a few. This year's theme, *Prophecy & Chance*, has allowed our curator, Holly Williams, to find a light-hearted (or, in some instances, dark-humoured) frame for the events of the year. It has also inspired our selection of an epidemiologist, a comedian and a data-analysing journalist, alongside talented thinkers, researchers and curators, to be judges of 2021's Political Cartoonist of the Year award.

We are delighted that journalist Karen Middleton is guest-curating our second 'In Focus' section. This important new addition to the onsite exhibition offers a chance to revisit an issue of significance: Australia's 20-year involvement in the war in Afghanistan. Middleton's unique insights draw on three trips to Afghanistan where she was embedded with the Australian Defence Force, and her current roles as Canberra-based author, panellist and political commentator. She and Holly Williams discussed how our cartoonists have covered the year's big issues.

As *Behind the Lines* continues to provide a creative and accessible overview of the political year that was, we hope it reminds you — once again — of the invaluable work artists play in capturing the moments and unravelling the spin.

Above: Badiucao
#HelpAfghanistanNow
Self-published
16 August 2021

REINVENTING THE WHEEL (OF FORTUNE)

How political cartoonists are adapting and surviving in a changing world

Lucien Leon

Cartoonists and scholars have been prophesying the death of political cartooning for decades. They're looking largely at the United States, and the decimation of the ranks of staff editorial cartoonists wrought by syndication and editorial censorship. This nation of 330 million people is home to a newspaper industry that at its peak employed approximately 2000 cartoonists, but now employs around 20.

Australia's highly concentrated newspaper ownership and the esteem in which cartoonists are generally held by newspaper editors have helped avoid a similar horror show here. Nonetheless, our political cartoonists are not immune to other, global threats and their ranks continue to shrink. As the public gravitates towards social media as a news source, the newspaper industry as a whole is struggling to retain readership. The digitisation of newspapers has deprived cartoonists of prized op-ed-page real estate and the once prominent editorial cartoon now languishes in the backwater of the digital image gallery. The rise of talk show satire and partisan comedians further encroaches on the cartoonist's traditional satirical space, which has shifted from a static medium to an increasingly audiovisual one.

The news is not all bad. Though the cultural, economic and technological disruption brought by the arrival of the internet has permanently changed our world, the political cartooning tradition has a proclivity for reinvention. From hand-engraving to photo-engraving, colour printing to digital image manipulation, cartoonists have consistently and enthusiastically adopted new technologies, techniques and contexts. It was a political cartoonist, for example, who created Australia's first publicly screened animations. From 1912 to 1918, Harry Julius's *Cartoons of the Moment* combined live-action film, lightning sketching and stop-motion animation in a series of satirical political vignettes prefixed to *Australasian Gazette* newsreels. (In a particularly delightful and prophetic clip, Julius predicts the miniskirt trend 45 years ahead of its time.)

This year's Political Cartoonist of the Year exemplifies the same spirit of technical and creative agility. Glen Le Lievre's animated GIFs showcase the best qualities of political cartoons in a digital moving-image format that is exclusive to the web browser. The seamless, looping structure of these images amplifies the poignancy and indignation residing in Le Lievre's powerful metaphors.

Le Lievre also demonstrates the entrepreneurial toolkit that today's cartoonists need to develop and maintain in order to survive in a gig economy dominated by short-term and casual contracts. Building and sustaining an audience demands an active online engagement with readers via the full suite of ubiquitous social media platforms — Twitter, Facebook, YouTube, Instagram and Pinterest — while an alternative revenue stream is facilitated by a Patreon subscription promising early or exclusive access to original content, and 'merch' in the

SYNCHRONIZED SINKING

captions or labels, memes capture many of the satirical and rhetorical elements of conventional cartoons.

We should be careful: the very characteristics that make memes powerful tools for activism — simplified graphics, anonymous creation and unregulated replication — also make them ideal vehicles for propaganda and misinformation. The circulation of memes has been shown to have directly contributed to the democratic crisis that enveloped the United States in the wake of the 2020 presidential election. Closer to home, memes were a key component of the 'Death Tax' campaign that aided the Coalition's victory in the 2019 federal election. When it comes to memes, filtering the dross from the inspired demands informed engagement from the consumer, who, without the benefit of journalistic context, may or may not be able to discern fact from fiction and sincerity from satire.

Cartoons continue to provoke, delight, amuse and inform us. We see the evidence for this in retweets, letters to the editor, and (occasionally) complaints to the Press Council. The tradition is not dying — merely evolving. But the outlook for the profession remains fragile, so think about adopting a political cartoonist today. 'Friend' them on Facebook, follow them on Instagram, retweet them on Twitter and buy their T-shirts. Supporting our artists provides our best chance of ensuring that we continue to enjoy their insightful, illuminating and downright funny drawings well into the future ... and prove the prophets of doom wrong once again.

form of original prints, signed copies and gift paraphernalia.

These platforms have also helped democratise political cartooning by equipping everyday users with the tools to produce and disseminate their own graphic satire. Over the last decade or so, political memes have captured the public's imagination as a grassroots iteration of the political cartoon. Comprising photographic or cartoon imagery and often overlayed with pithy

Lucien Leon is an independent researcher who writes on political satire and contemporary new media. His publications include 'Cartoons, memes and videos', in Anika Gauja, Marian Sawer and Marian Simms (eds), *Morrison's Miracle: The 2019 Australian Federal Election* (2020); and 'The evolution of political cartooning in the new media age: Cases from Australia, the USA and the UK', in Jessica Milner Davis (ed.), *Satire and Politics: The Interplay of Heritage and Practice* (2017). He was a guest judge for *Behind the Lines 2021: Prophecy & Chance*.

Left: Glen Le Lievre
Synchronized Sinking
Patreon
28 July 2021
From the exhibition's
A Sporting Chance
section

Above: Glen Le Lievre
Free at Last
Patreon
11 October 2021
From the exhibition's
Consulting the
Oracle section

2021: A YEAR OF FURY AND FATIGUE

Behind the Lines curator Holly Williams sat down with journalist Karen Middleton for a lively discussion about the big issues of 2021 and five cartoons that captured them.

Holly Williams (HW): What words sum up the year for you?

Karen Middleton (KM): I would say fatigue and fury. Because we're over it. We thought the pandemic would be over by now and we're starting to get angry at a whole lot of things: at the circumstances that we're in, the way the response has been managed, and at the governments, plural, that we blame for these and other problems. The things that they're doing under cover of the pandemic, or not doing — some of those are making people angry as well.

Trust in state and federal governments shot up last year because people had to rely on them to make things right for us as the pandemic began. But I think the underlying lack of trust in and concern about governments is still there, and a year later that has surged back. It's now magnified by the COVID experience and it's connected to a whole lot of other doubts Australians might've had: about individual politicians, leaders on both sides of politics at the federal and state level, and other institutions that we were forced to put our faith in that we might now feel are not necessarily doing right by us.

HW: David Pope's *Gaslight Station* (top and p. 68) tackles one of the central issues of the year.

KM: This cleverly encapsulates two issues that came together around the vaccine distribution. One is the sense that the government wasn't well enough organised and didn't get enough

vaccine for us in the first place. And then came the messaging from the government and the role that played in how people felt about vaccination. This cartoon sums that up nicely.

HW: And the Prime Minister running a 'gaslight station'?

KM: 'Gaslighting' is doing or saying something to create a false impression or narrative and make whoever's being targeted doubt themselves, or even think they're losing their grip on reality. This image merges public frustrations around the vaccine rollout with a couple of well-ventilated observations that critics make of the Prime Minister — that he changes his story to suit a new circumstance and avoids taking responsibility for mistakes.

HW: Broelman's straight to the point cartoon *The Canberra Bubble* (overleaf and p. 41) was published on 1 March but could apply to a number of headline-making events across the year.

THE CANBERRA BUBBLE

KM: Well, speaking as someone who's inside that bubble, I think this searingly captures the attitude to women — around Parliament House and more broadly — that's been dragged into the daylight this year. This particular physical bubble depicts not only a male-dominant environment but also the pressure on people inside it.

The issue gained focus with the appointment of Grace Tame as Australian of the Year. When that coalesced with Brittany Higgins' allegations, it was a flashpoint. Parliament House became the symbol of what's wrong with our attitudes to women and people converged in rallies around the country, but particularly in front of that building, to make their voices heard.

This cartoon comments on the unconsciousness of those attitudes, the fact that they're so normalised in Parliament House that some people haven't even realised they are hermetically sealed from the thinking outside. It became an unavoidable issue for our political leaders and women suddenly had a collective voice. We could see how this affects people in our parliament. This affects people in our schools and in our wider community. It affects a lot of people all the time and, really, we should focus on it.

I think it's also highlighted the importance of public discourse — of good-quality journalism, of depicting things like this in cartoons, and of crystallising ideas in the public mind, in the public domain, and not just dealing with things in private. There's a place for dealing with some things in private, but to achieve social and attitudinal change, it has to be public.

HW: There have been a number of cartoons about changes to Labor's policy position and the perception that it's walked away from some of its core principles. What stands out to me in Jon Kudelka's *Drover's Dog* (below and p. 24) are the faceless men doing the training. What's your take?

KW: The Drover's Dog School is a reference to 1983 when Bill Hayden suggested a drover's

EVACUEES..

David Rowe
Evacuees
Australian Financial Review
20 August 2021

dog could win the election, called the day he was swapped out for Bob Hawke. So, there's an implication here about Anthony Albanese, about whether he should be doing better as leader than he is, and who is really in charge. The 'faceless men' is another historical reference to backroom people pulling the strings.

Under his predecessor Bill Shorten, Labor made itself a very big target with some controversial policies that the Coalition was able to attack, successfully. Under Anthony Albanese they've gone the other way, made themselves a very small target, produced fewer policies and are now being seen by some people, who might traditionally be inclined to support them, as not standing up for enough, as standing for nothing. This image is quite a biting summary of the frustrations being expressed on the progressive side of politics, I think.

HW: David Rowe's *Evacuees* (above) is one of the year's standout cartoons both for the sophistication of composition and the palpable emotion it conveys. Your book on Australia's involvement in Afghanistan was published a decade ago and you were embedded there with Australian troops. This cartoon must cut pretty close to the bone.

KM: Well, we've seen the official end of a 20-year Afghanistan war in the most terrible, appalling way really. Rowe's cartoon sums that up grotesquely and beautifully, because the evacuees we see here are not the real evacuees, the ones that we saw at Kabul airport and falling from the undercarriages of planes. These evacuees are politicians getting out for their own reasons. Interestingly, Scott Morrison's the first to flee. Perhaps that symbolises the closure of our embassy earlier in the year, which angered the American government and was seen as precipitating problems in Kabul more broadly. But here you see Joe Biden and Boris Johnson also heading over and out and leaving behind all the women of Afghanistan imprisoned.

It's quite a profound analysis, in a single image, of what has occurred this year in Afghanistan. We don't know the fate of the woman behind the veil. But we can see the fate of the politicians — they're cutting loose. I think that we all have this on our consciences now. The United States and Britain are insisting, 'We are doing this in the best interests of our countries'. Rowe's use of the flag, as the knotted linen out the window — the classic jailbreak cliché — suggests it's patriotism they're clinging to as they make their escape.

HW: Rowe's central figure is set against the sky; she's not embedded in a landscape. There's a sense of a geography of everywhere.

KM: There are two things that strike me. It's the grief in the eyes of the woman, the sadness and despair, and it's the beauty of the colours in the background. Afghanistan is a bewitchingly beautiful country. Very stark, quite brutal, but also gentle and glorious in its colour from dawn through daylight to dusk. That is captured here but also obscured a bit by the political activity. You still get the sense of the landscape through the colour, but the outline of it is unclear. All you see clearly is the sadness of the woman left behind.

HW: Cartoonists relish depicting Barnaby Joyce. Cathy Wilcox has risen to the occasion yet again with *Who Pays?* (right and p. 118).

KM: Yes, she has put Barnaby Joyce right in front of the kids, explaining something that they probably don't understand, but they are going to be either the victims or beneficiaries of, depending on what this guy with the angry fist-pumping demeanour decides with his Nationals colleagues. This shows the competing constituencies in this debate. Here, Joyce is talking about his party's political constituency, the rural people he worries will have to pay the greatest price in the short term for action on climate change. But he's speaking to the ultimate constituents, the children, who will pay the greatest price in the long term for our failure to act until now.

It also depicts the way climate change has been discussed in this country for 15 years, in the sense that it's a global issue, it's our whole planet's future, but we have persistently seen it in terms of domestic politics. Wilcox shows the smallness of our debate contrasting with the bigness of the issue and its implications. It has

taken a change of administration in the United States to change the global dynamic on this. And we, as a country, are now being forced to do something that we should have been able to see was necessary generations ago. This cartoon nicely captures all the layers of that debate, the short-sightedness of it and what's at stake.

HW: It's been a year with examples of strong public pushback against what we've just gone along with. Hopefully if the pandemic's been good for anything, it's been for people to be more proactive, more participatory at some level.

KM: There's been a sense of both public frustration and empowerment. There is a message in there to our political leaders that they need to improve their engagement with the people they are supposed to be serving.

Almost all the cartoons we've discussed transcend transactional politics: going to

principles and obligations and our moral compass in the case of Afghanistan; community safety and community benefit in terms of the COVID approach; the future of the planet; half the population and the way the other half interacts with them; and the alternative government and the standards to which it is being held. So, there is a sense, not just of pushback in a practical way, but of a return to matters of principle in what is otherwise an increasingly transactional approach to politics. And I think that's been an interesting theme of the year. Whether that hangs around and lives past these issues of 2021 is unclear. But I hope it does.

Karen Middleton is a Canberra-based journalist, author, panellist and political commentator. She is currently chief political correspondent for *The Saturday Paper*. As SBS TV's chief political correspondent, Middleton made three trips to Afghanistan where she was embedded with the Australian Defence Force. Middleton has written two books: *An Unwinnable War: Australia in Afghanistan* (2011) and *Albanese: Telling it Straight* (2016). She guest-curated *In Focus: Afghanistan*, an onsite component of *Behind the Lines 2021* featuring cartoons covering the past 20 years of Australia's involvement in the war in Afghanistan.

Holly Williams is a Sydney-based freelance curator and director of The Curators' Department. This is her third time curating *Behind the Lines*, following 2017's *Behind the Lines: Three-Ring Circus* and *Behind the Lines 2020: A Dog's Breakfast*.

PROPHECY & CHANCE

Behind the Lines 2021 is rummaging in the fortune-teller's chest for a crystal ball. Just as predictive models have become ever-present in the news cycle, the exhibition's theme, *Prophecy & Chance*, acknowledges our discomfort with uncertainty and our quest to know what the future holds.

Peering into the swirling mists of the 'Canberra bubble', our talented political cartoonists have illuminated the complex issues of 2021's 'new normal' — a year peppered with big reports, unexpected outcomes and floundering forecasts. From COVID-19 case numbers to house prices and employment levels, 2021 was a year to expect the unexpected.

Alongside the all-too-familiar stories of leadership jockeying and funding scandals, a handful of issues dominated the headlines: the pandemic and vaccine rollout, the treatment of women in our democracy, climate change and government policy. Luckily our artists were on hand to read the tea leaves and cut through the spin. In addition to some talented familiar faces led by our Political Cartoonist of the Year, Glen Le Lievre, *Behind the Lines* is introducing several first-time contributors into the mix who reflect our dynamic democracy. We hope your time consulting these 'oracles' helps you make sense of, and maybe even laugh at, 2021's mixed fortunes.

GLEN LE LIEVRE

Political Cartoonist of the Year

Judges singled out Glen Le Lievre for his ability to wordlessly express complex issues and emotions. In 2020 he broke new ground as the first cartoonist to show digital works in *Behind the Lines*. Based in Sydney, Le Lievre publishes online through Patreon, and in the *Australian Financial Review* and the *Australian*, among others. He shared the following tips for future cartoonists:

Do 1001 bad drawings

The great American animator Chuck Jones once said: 'Every artist has thousands of bad drawings inside them and the only way to get rid of them is to draw them out'. Honestly, you'll be surprised at how quickly and eagerly those little stinkers want to leap from your brain, down your arm, through your pen, onto the page and straight into the trash. Every bad drawing makes you better. (Or if you do happen to be reading this in the future, every bad drawing makes your robot better.)

Be like Pizza Rat

Remember that meme of a rat dragging a slice of pizza down the steps into the New York subway? Well that's exactly the sort of tenacity, business savvy and fondness for cold pizza you need to be a working cartoonist. Conference drawing, T-shirts, greeting cards, crowdfunding, Kickstarter, dancing for nickels, anything with

pineapple topping: all these little morsels make up a tasty whole. So take whatever work you can get your ratty little paws on and drag it down those steps and into your burrow. (Apologies to any cartoonist who actually does live in a subway burrow.)

'Only what's necessary'
… is the title of Chip Kidd's book about *Peanuts* creator Charles M Schulz's change in design after his cartoon strip was reduced to the size of a postage stamp. 'Sparky' Schulz simply stopped drawing anything that didn't support a joke. Pretty good advice, with attention spans heading downhill faster than a slice of pizza being dragged down subway steps. Or as many editors are wont to say, 'Make your point, keep it simple and get out'. (Note, while editors will often omit the bits about making your point and keeping it simple, they always remember the part about getting out.)

Better animation through ball gowns
If you're not a younger version of Anne Telnaes (animator/editorial cartoonist at the *Washington Post*), you may end up being tempted by an antiquated backwater of Photoshop aptly called Timeline. (Think Monty Python's Terry Gilliam moving bits of cut out paper around, but done digitally.) Then imagine the horror of learning you actually need to draw about six different pairs of legs just to make a drawing walk. Six! Then realising that must be why Gilliam animated so many men in long dresses. (Thank heavens the Catholic church is forever in the news.)

Don't die from exposure
Value your work, even if others can't, don't or won't. Say you apply for a gig at an online news media outlet. Sadly, their budget is so unapologetically tiny that you have to drop your rate to roughly one can of creamed corn per drawing. But hey, you get to keep calling yourself a cartoonist and they get some quite nice GIFs and cartoons for the price of an intern who makes coffee. An absolute win-win. (Right up until you're fired because they think the money would be better spent on an intern who makes coffee.)

Political Cartoonist of the Year judges in 2021 were Casey Briggs, Marcus Hughes, Daryl Karp, Lucien Leon, Nanette Louchart-Fletcher, Mary-Louise McLaws, Steph Tisdell and Holly Williams.

Facing page: Glen Le Lievre
Self-portrait
15 October 2021

Above left: Glen Le Lievre
Future Cartoonist
10 November 2021

POLITICAL LIFE LINES

Palmistry and the art of political survival

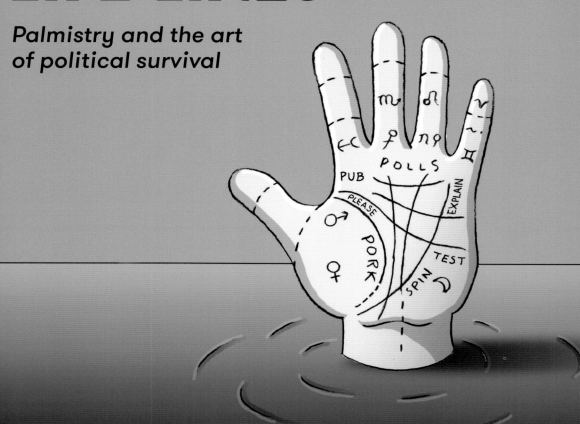

A Cabinet reshuffle, an uncomfortable compromise and a move to the backbench are all pretty standard stuff for parliament. Yet the return to party leadership of Barnaby Joyce — the cartoonists' darling and one of Australia's most resilient politicians — still felt surprisingly fast following his departure in 2018. In other news, two former prime ministers (from different sides of the aisle) joined forces to challenge a media baron, and the Leader of the Opposition took heat for a policy backflip.

Jim Pavlidis
The PM of No Responsibility
The Sydney Morning Herald/The Age
23 August 2021

Cathy Wilcox
Daddy, What Did YOU Do?
The Sydney Morning Herald/The Age
8 September 2021

Jon Kudelka
Drover's Dog
The Saturday Paper
3 July 2021

WITH PUBS REOPENING, MALCOLM WAS BACK ON THE USUAL...

Warren Brown
Sour Grapes
The Daily Telegraph
30 September 2021

David Rowe
Political Actors
Australian Financial Review
13 April 2021

Cathy Wilcox
Free Speech, Baby!
The Sydney Morning Herald/The Age
12 October 2021

Glen Le Lievre
Human Shield
Patreon
22 July 2021

Mark Knight
An Immune Response
Herald Sun
5 August 2021

Matt Golding
Bin Night
The Sydney Morning Herald/The Age
23 June 2021

Alan Moir
One of these Days You'll Push Me Too Far
The Sydney Morning Herald/The Age
26 June 2021

John Shakespeare
Clive Palmer Erases Himself
The Sydney Morning Herald/The Age
2 August 2021

John Shakespeare
The Wheels of Justice Roll Along
The Sydney Morning Herald/The Age
5 August 2021

Cathy Wilcox
Blind Trust
The Sydney Morning Herald/The Age
16 September 2021

David Pope
Home to Bilo
The Canberra Times
12 June 2021

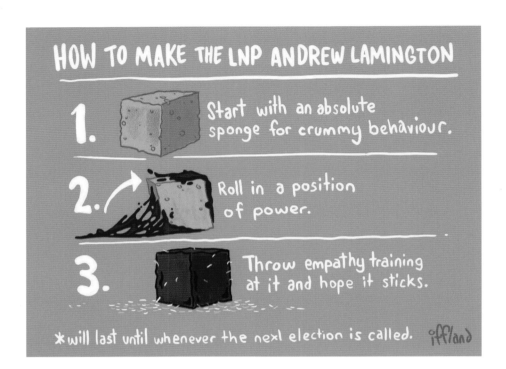

HOW TO MAKE THE LNP ANDREW LAMINGTON

1. Start with an absolute sponge for crummy behaviour.

2. Roll in a position of power.

3. Throw empathy training at it and hope it sticks.

*will last until whenever the next election is called.

Edmund Iffland
How to Make the LNP Andrew Lamington
Self-published
1 April 2021 (this version 20 October 2021)

Glen Le Lievre
Gold Standard
Patreon
7 October 2021

THE EMPRESS

*Tarot, toxic workplaces
and time for change*

Allegations and scandals swirled around Parliament House. Across the country, women spoke up, empowering others to come forward. Thousands marched, calling for an end to sexism, misogyny, corruption and damaging workplace cultures. Muted reactions and a campaign misfire caught the cartoonists' attention. Showing just how slow progress can be, an elite club, whose members include former prime ministers and governors-general, continued its ban on women as members.

Fiona Katauskas
Dream Jobs
Eureka Street
9 March 2021

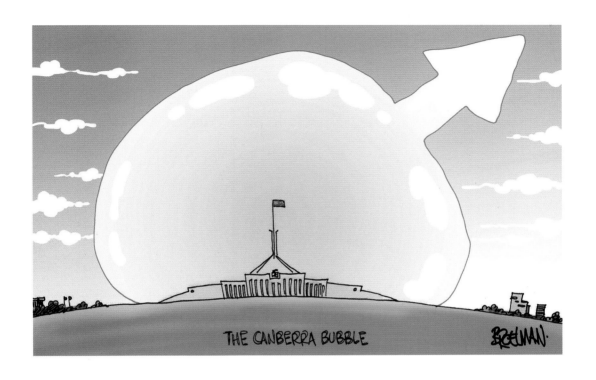

Peter Broelman
The Canberra Bubble
The Canberra Times
1 March 2021

David Rowe
It's Not Just the Economy ... Stupid
Australian Financial Review
4 March 2021

Peter Broelman
Inquiring Minds
The Canberra Times
26 March 2021

Brett Lethbridge
Little Help
The Courier-Mail
15 April 2021

Glen Le Lievre
Dazed and Confused
Patreon
21 April 2021

Fiona Katauskas
Window of Opportunity
Eureka Street
16 March 2021

Harry Bruce
A Triumph for Democracy
Townsville Bulletin
15 March 2021

David Pope
Grace
The Canberra Times
4 March 2021

The PM has made some new appointments, to show just how serious he is about changing the culture for women in Australia. To name a few:

Marise Payne

MINISTER FOR KEEPING QUIET

Amanda Stoker

MINISTER FOR NOTHING TO SEE HERE

Michaelia Cash

MINISTER FOR LOOK OVER THERE

Andrew Laming

SPECIAL ENVOY FOR ZERO CONSEQUENCES.

Wilcox

Cathy Wilcox
Serious about Women
The Sydney Morning Herald/The Age
31 March 2021

Members of the Australian Club vote to allow women
to come to the table in the only way that does not
offend their core values.

Megan Herbert
The Australian Club
Self-published
18 June 2021

David Pope
Returned to Sender
The Canberra Times
14 April 2021

A SPORTING CHANCE

Politics and spectator sports

Sports commentators and political cartoonists share a love of metaphors, mishaps and exaggeration. 2021's headline sporting events gave both professions a workout. From tennis and cycling to the much-needed distraction of the Tokyo Olympics, our competitive spirit provided cartoonists with visual gags for a range of issues, from Labor policies to the vaccine rollout. Beyond the goings-on in Canberra, a new champion was celebrated. In Melbourne, political cartooning took to the street, or to be more specific, the tennis court.

Mark Knight
Team Australia
Herald Sun
24 July 2021

Fiona Katauskas
Going for Gold
Eureka Street
5 August 2021

Andrew Dyson
Degree of Difficulty
The Sydney Morning Herald/The Age
29 July 2021

David Rowe
Low Bar Olympians
Australian Financial Review
3 August 2021

Brett Lethbridge
Boom!
The Courier-Mail
22 July 2021

Chris Downes
Pride of Place
Hobart Mercury
12 July 2021

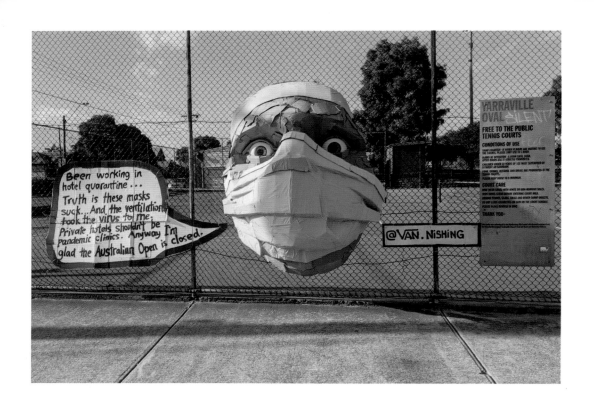

Van T Rudd
The Closed Australian Open
Installed Anderson Street, Yarraville, Victoria
12 February 2021

John Shakespeare
Aussie Aussie Aussie for Some
The Sydney Morning Herald/The Age
18 May 2021

David Pope
Rollout de Vax
The Canberra Times
29 June 2021

Fiona Katauskas
Missing in Opposition
Eureka Street
19 October 2021

ROLL(OUT) OF THE DICE

Promises and pitfalls of governing in a pandemic

The federal government's aim to vaccinate the nation faced a perfect storm of unexpected side effects, supply issues and a highly contagious new virus variant. Armchair experts honed their skills on increasingly detailed COVID-19 reporting. Amid bad headlines and finger pointing, lockdowns spread across the country while outspoken MPs undermined public health messaging, causing headaches for the government. The numbers 70 and 80 became shorthand for freedom.

Jon Kudelka
The Fumble
The Saturday Paper
13 February 2021

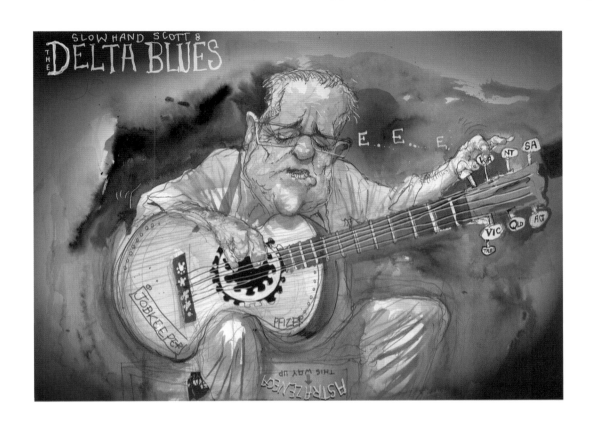

David Rowe
The Delta Blues
Australian Financial Review
17 July 2021

David Pope
Gaslight Station
The Canberra Times
27 May 2021

Brett Lethbridge
Lord and Saviour
The Courier-Mail
14 July 2021

Warren Brown
All That Glitters
The Daily Telegraph
28 June 2021

Fiona Katauskas
Bad Call
Eureka Street
13 July 2021

Mark Knight
The Vaccine Rollout
Herald Sun
2 July 2021

Glen Le Lievre
Full House
The Australian
21 September 2021

73

Meg O'Shea
Phonecall with Aunty
Self-published
2 August 2021

Warren Brown
Impact
The Daily Telegraph
3 September 2021

Johannes Leak
Home Stretch
The Australian
3 July 2021

Matt Golding
Cave Dwellers
The Sydney Morning Herald/The Age
27 August 2021

Harry Bruce
Don't Be Afraid
Townsville Bulletin
12 August 2021

Jon Kudelka
Homeopathic Remedy
The Saturday Paper
23 September 2021

Glen Le Lievre
Pretzel
Australian Financial Review
4 September 2021

Mark David
Opening up the Pool
Independent Australia
30 August 2021

WHEEL OF FORTUNE

Winners and losers in a post-pandemic economy

Money talks. Here, money-themed cartoons give a visual oration of the year's political and social issues. In 2021 we saw the impact of the pandemic on budgets, debt levels and political party positions. As self-made billionaires indulged in a space race, the economic cost of climate change loomed. Questions of management and oversight came to the fore. Wealth inequality, support for the vulnerable and our old friend, the pork barrel, made an appearance.

WHIPLASH ECONOMICS

Matt Davidson
Whiplash Economics
The Sydney Morning Herald/The Age
4 September 2021

Matt Davidson
The Bigger Picture
The Sydney Morning Herald/The Age
6 March 2021

Harry Bruce
Conversion Road to Recovery
Townsville Bulletin
12 May 2021

Matt Golding
Budget Butter
The Sydney Morning Herald/The Age
18 May 2021

Matt Golding
Inheritance
The Sydney Morning Herald/The Age
17 May 2021

DOUGHNUT ECONOMICS!

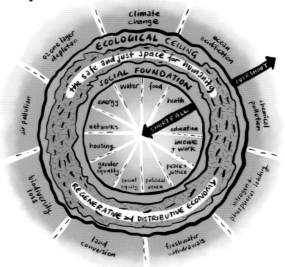

Sarah Firth
Doughnut Dayz
Self-published
11 November 2020

Andrew Dyson
Home Stretch
The Sydney Morning Herald/The Age
10 March 2021

Jon Kuldelka
The View from the Top
The Saturday Paper
24 July 2021

David Rowe
NSW PM
Australian Financial Review
15 July 2021

Cathy Wilcox
Cash for Votes
The Sydney Morning Herald/The Age
4 August 2021

Reg Lynch
Department of Consequences
The Sun-Herald
11 April 2021

THE POLITICS OF ENVY...

Alan Moir
The Politics of Envy
The Sydney Morning Herald
11 September 2021

Glen Le Lievre
Blind Trust
Patreon
10 September 2021

David Rowe
Prices on Request
Australian Financial Review
7 October 2021

MARS RETROGRADE

*Astrological forecasts
and the god of war*

From time to time, Mars appears to move backwards across the sky. Astronomers know this to be an optical illusion. Astrologers, however, see it as symbolic, linked to war, action and self-assertion. The astrologers' take on Mars is the thread linking these cartoons together. This year, democracy, international relations and our defence force were in the spotlight. Tragedies here and overseas reminded us that 2021 also marked two grim anniversaries: the 20th anniversary of 9/11, which triggered Australia's longest war, and the 30th anniversary of the report of the Royal Commission into Aboriginal Deaths in Custody.

Greg 'Smithy' Smith
The View from Lincoln Memorial
The Sunday Times (Perth)
8 January 2021

Warren Brown
Twenty Years
The Daily Telegraph
11 September 2021

Warren Brown
Incoming
The Daily Telegraph
26 April 2021

Mark Knight
You're My Au-Pair
Herald Sun
17 August 2021

David Pope
The Drums of War
The Canberra Times
29 April 2021

David Rowe
At the Going down of the Sun
Australian Financial Review
13 April 2021

Andrew Weldon
Trade with China
The Big Issue
16 May 2021

John Spooner
Port of Darwin
The Australian
5 May 2021

Johannes Leak
Grown-Ups Club
The Australian
17 September 2021

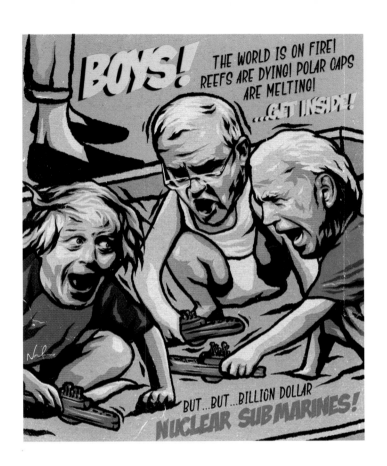

Nordacious (James Hillier)
Boys And Their Dumb Toys
Self-published
17 September 2021

Jon Kudelka
Sparkling Submersibles
The Saturday Paper
18 September 2021

Fiona Katauskas
The Heart of the Matter
Eureka Street
8 June 2021

Danny Eastwood
Black Lives Matter: Black Deaths in Custody Since 1991
Koori Mail
7 April 2021

HOW TO CHOOSE A GOOD DAY FOR A CELEBRATION:

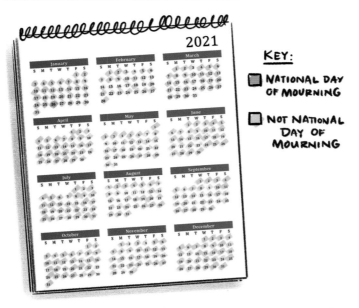

Made by @meganjherbert on Boon Wurrung/Bunurong land.

Megan Herbert
Change the Date
Self-published
26 January 2021

BAD OMENS

*Impending doom and signs
impossible to ignore*

One of 2021's biggest reports forecast a bleak climate future. For decades, cartoonists have been reflecting on the science, debates and political posturing that mark global warming. As experts' warnings become more dire and more urgent, cartoonists have found new ways to illustrate this familiar territory. A cartoon about the floods in eastern Australia captures the mood of the nation, while high-vis vests, VR goggles and a buggy whip warehouse provoke a chuckle.

Johannes Leak
Floods
The Australian
22 March 2021

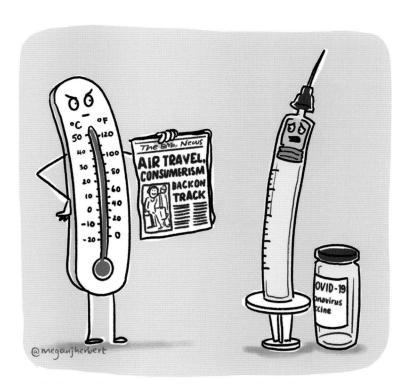

"When they said they wanted to be saved, I assumed they were talking long term."

Megan Herbert
Save Us from Ourselves
(with the Thermometer and Syringe)
Self-published
20 August 2021

Cathy Wilcox
Who Pays?
The Sydney Morning Herald/The Age
18 August 2021

Phil Somerville
Headspace
Line of Thought
10 August 2021

First Dog on the Moon
Angry Climate Kids
The Guardian
3 September 2021

Jon Kudelka
Heritage Tours
The Saturday Paper
20 May 2021

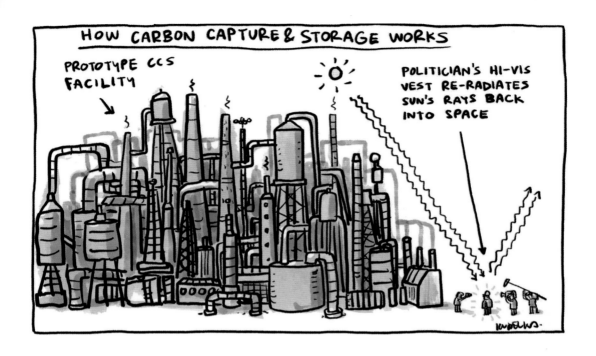

Jon Kudelka
Burying Disbelief
The Australian
24 April 2021

Glen Le Lievre
The Science of PCS (Politician Capture & Storage)
Patreon
4 November 2021

John Spooner
Renewed Energy
The Australian
19 April 2021

Johannes Leak
Snake Oil Sales
The Australian
22 April 2021

Matt Golding
Australia's Climate Action
The Sydney Morning Herald/The Age
27 October 2021

Alan Moir
Angus and Climate Change
The Sydney Morning Herald/The Age
20 March 2021

David Rowe
Beautiful One Day … Blindsided the Next
Australian Financial Review
23 June 2021

Jon Kudelka
Reef-Coloured Glasses
The Saturday Paper
26 June 2021

CONSULTING THE ORACLE

How we live now

With their poignant reflections on our post-pandemic world, artists are the oracles helping us navigate our 'new normal'. For millions of us caught in the extended lockdowns of 2021, the images of faraway loved ones, overweight pets or a simple drawing of a footpath resonate in a way that would have seemed unimaginable in 2019. The exhibition's first QR code cartoon sits alongside the Museum of Nice Things and a world on hold.

Chris Downes
Connection Error
Hobart *Mercury*
31 May 2021

First Dog on the Moon
Museum of Nice Things
The Guardian
14 May 2021

Andrew Weldon
Books Explaining the News for Kids
The Big Issue
4 March 2021

'We've moved a few things around. Travel books are in the Fantasy section, Politics is in Sci-Fi, and Epidemiology is in Self-Help. Good luck.'

Megan Herbert
New Categories
Self-published
16 November 2020

Matt Golding
Armchair Experts
The Sydney Morning Herald/The Age
21 September 2021

Chris Downes
Abstract Zeneca
Hobart Mercury
9 August 2021

11:15 am

Elyce Phillips
Waiting for Presser
Self-published
12 Februrary 2021

Judy Kuo
Lockdown Mood 6
Self-published
13 August 2021

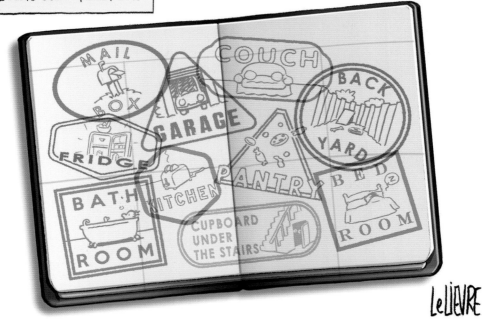

Glen Le Lievre
The Lockdown Passport
Australian Financial Review
1 September 2021

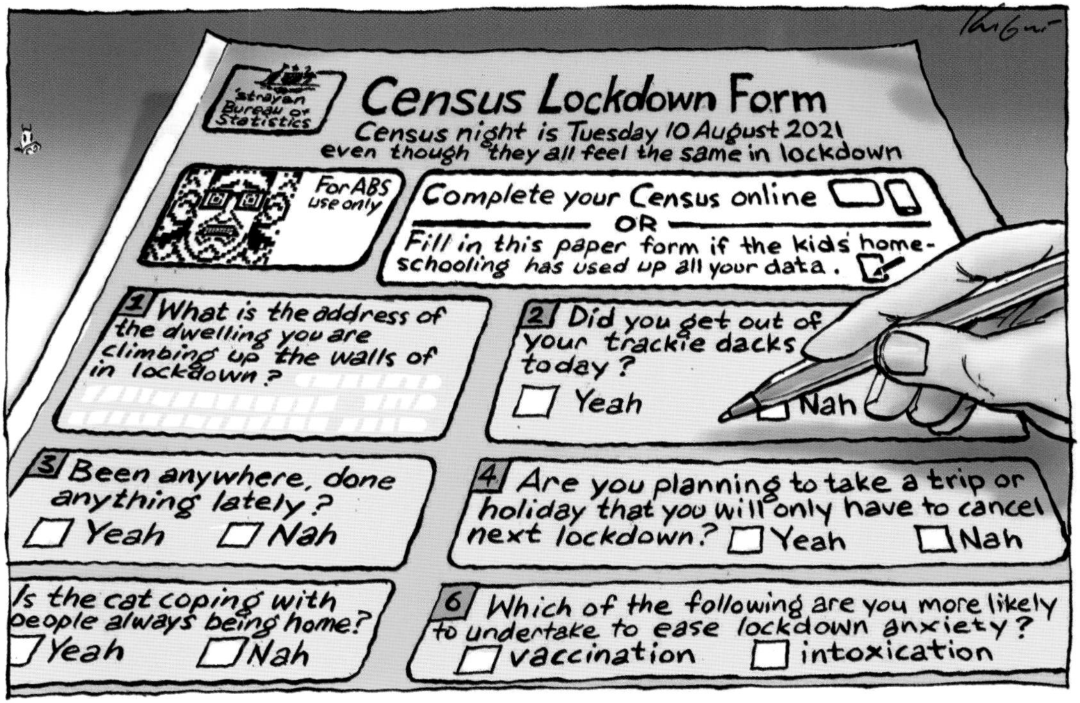

Mark Knight
Census
Herald Sun
11 August 2021

Cathy Wilcox
Lower Your Expectations
The Sydney Morning Herald/The Age
20 August 2021

Andrew Dyson
Bubble Wrap
The Sydney Morning Herald/The Age
3 June 2021

(Scan codes to enter illustration)

Simon Letch
Track Record
The Sydney Morning Herald/The Age
10 September 2021

Glen Le Lievre
The Long Goodbye
Patreon
29 April 2021

About the Artists

Badiucao
Badiucao is a Chinese–Australian political cartoonist, artist and rights activist, whose work addresses a variety of social and political issues. He is regarded as one of China's most prolific and well-known political cartoonists. In 2019 Badiucao won the Robert Russell Courage in Cartooning Award and the following year the Human Rights Foundation named him joint winner of the Vaclav Havel International Prize for Creative Dissent.

Peter Broelman
Peter Broelman is an Adelaide-based freelance cartoonist and illustrator, whose nationally syndicated cartoons appear in a wide range of publications, including the *Canberra Times*, *Geelong Advertiser* and *Sunshine Coast Daily*. He has won three Stanley Awards for his editorial cartoons (2004, 2005 and 2009) and has twice been named Gold Stanley Cartoonist of the Year (2005 and 2009).

Warren Brown
Warren Brown, who signs his cartoons 'Warren', has been an editorial cartoonist since 1986, and his work appears regularly in Sydney's *Daily Telegraph*. He is also a television presenter, vintage car enthusiast and motoring columnist. Brown has won three Stanley Awards for best political cartoonist (1997, 1998 and 1999).

Harry Bruce
A born-and-bred north Queenslander, Bruce is a prolific artist who has been cartooning for regional newspapers in Queensland for more than 30 years. He often creates up to five cartoons a day, and his work has appeared in newspapers from Cairns to Longreach and most towns in-between.

Gaynor Alma Cardew
Gaynor Cardew was a Canberra-based printmaker, sculptor and cartoonist, who signed her work 'Gaynor'. Her cartoons appeared in a range of publications, including government reports and newsletters, privately printed books and, occasionally, the *Canberra Times*. Several volumes of her own cartoons were also published. She died in 1999, aged 47.

Mark David
Mark David is a Queensland-based cartoonist, illustrator and photographer, with more than 20 years' experience in cartooning. He is widely published and has won several awards for his work. David's work has appeared in the *Australian Financial Review*, *Bulletin* and *Sydney Morning Herald* and he now works for *Independent Australia*.

Matt Davidson
Melbourne-based Matt Davidson's cartoons have appeared in the *Age* for more than 20 years. In 2008 he won the Melbourne Press Club's Quill Award for Best Illustration.

Chris Downes

Based in Tasmania, Chris Downes regularly draws for the Hobart *Mercury*. He has also created works for MoAD and for the *Lore* podcast. Downes works for the Museum of Old and New Art (Mona), where he believes his mind is slowly being corrupted. That didn't stop him from creating the book *Mona's Ark*, a zoological appreciation of art from Mona's collection. Downes won a Stanley Award in 2015.

Andrew Dyson

Andrew Dyson began working as a cartoonist for the Melbourne *Herald*, moving to the *Sunday Age* in 1989, and then to the *Age* 10 years later. His work also appears regularly in the *Sydney Morning Herald*. Dyson has won Walkley Awards for cartooning (2004) and illustrations (2005).

Danny Eastwood

Danny Eastwood is a member of the Ngemba tribe of western New South Wales. He is a painter, illustrator and regular cartoonist for the *Koori Mail*. Eastwood has created public artworks and murals in Sydney and has won many awards, including, twice, NAIDOC NSW Aboriginal Artist of the Year.

First Dog on the Moon

First Dog on the Moon (who used to be known as Andrew Marlton) has been a full-time cartoonist since 2007, first at *Crikey* and then, since 2014, at the *Guardian Australia*. He has also written and illustrated books and performed live on stage. Mr Onthemoon is a Walkley Award-winner and was MoAD's Political Cartoonist of the Year in 2011.

Sarah Firth

Based on Wurundjeri country, Sarah Firth is an Eisner-Award-winning cartoonist, a comic artist and writer, speaker and graphic recorder. Her work has been published by ABRAMS Books, ABC Arts, *Frankie Magazine*, *kuš!*, Graphic Mundi (Penn State University Press), Penguin Random House, Picador, Allen & Unwin, the *Nib*, Black Inc. and Routledge. She is currently working on her debut graphic novel.

Matt Golding

Melbourne-based Matt Golding has been cartooning for more than 25 years. He is currently political cartoonist for the *Age* and *Sunday Age*. A collection of his cartoons, *Three Second Thoughts*, was published in 2009. Golding has received a Walkley Award, eight Stanley Awards (including Best Single Gag Cartoon every year from 2005 to 2010) and, in 2018, was honoured as MoAD's Political Cartoonist of the Year.

Megan Herbert

Megan Herbert is an artist, writer and cartoonist whose work primarily deals with environmental and social justice issues. She has been writing for television and film, cartooning, live-drawing, designing products and creating children's books for 20 years. After 13 years living abroad (in the United Kingdom, Iceland and the Netherlands), she returned to Australia in 2020 to live on Victoria's Mornington Peninsula.

James Hillier

Brisbane-based artist James Hillier, also known as Nordacious, specialises in portraiture, creating work inspired by pop culture, Australiana, sociopolitical commentary and queer + camp. Hillier has had three solo exhibitions since 2015. His current project is a series of billboards drawing attention to Australia's track record on climate action for COP26, the United Nations Climate Change Conference in Glasgow in November 2021.

Edmund Iffland

Edmund Iffland is a freelance artist based in Sydney's inner west. Mostly working as a cartoonist, storyboard artist and graphic designer, Iffland is also a regular entrant in the Archibald Prize, with recent portraits of artist–activist Badiucao and satirists James Colley and Mark Humphries.

Fiona Katauskas

Sydneysider Fiona Katauskas has been a freelance cartoonist since 1997. Her work has appeared in a wide range of publications, including the *Sydney Morning Herald*, the *Australian*, the *Age*, *New Matilda* and *Eureka Street*. She is also the author and illustrator of *The Amazing True Story of How Babies Are Made* (2015).

Mark Knight

Mark Knight is a cartoonist for the Melbourne *Herald Sun*, having been the last editorial cartoonist for its predecessor, the *Herald*. He is also well-known in Melbourne for his AFL premiership posters. Knight is a much-awarded cartoonist, having received two Golden Quill Awards from the Melbourne Press Club, two Walkley Awards and two Stanley Awards. He was named MoAD's Political Cartoonist of the Year in 2014.

Jon Kudelka

A freelance cartoonist based in Hobart, Jon Kudelka regularly publishes in the Hobart *Mercury* and the *Saturday Paper*. He has been cartooning for more than 10 years — hence, he says, his haggard looks. Kudelka has won two Walkley Awards (2008 and 2018), a Stanley Award and several others recognising his talent. He has been MoAD's Political Cartoonist of the Year twice, in 2010 and 2019.

Judy Kuo

Judy Kuo is a visual artist and activist, living and working on Wurundjeri country. She is passionate about developing a politically energised art practice, particularly in areas of anti-racism, workers' rights and disability justice. The child of multiple generations of refugees, she is also an activist for refugee rights. Kuo has participated in projects for Diversity Arts Australia, Multicultural Arts Victoria, *demos journal* and local zines.

Johannes Leak

Johannes Leak is an artist, cartoonist and illustrator based in New South Wales. His cartoons appear regularly in the *Australian* and in *Tracks* surfing magazine. Leak also illustrates children's books and has been commissioned to paint the official portrait of former prime minister Tony Abbott.

Glen Le Lievre

Sydneysider Glen Le Lievre's cartoons and illustrations have appeared in the *Age*, the *Sydney Morning Herald*, *MAD*, *Private Eye*, *Reader's Digest*, the *New Yorker*, *Time* and the *Wall Street Journal*. He has also worked in comedy on radio and television. Le Lievre is MoAD's Political Cartoonist of the Year 2021. You can read more about his work on p. 18.

Simon Letch

Sydney-based Simon Letch is an illustrator whose works appear regularly in the *Age* and *Sydney Morning Herald*. He describes himself as a 'surfer at Bronte, cook at home'.

Brett Lethbridge

Brett Lethbridge is an artist, gallery owner and cartoonist. His editorial cartoons have appeared in the *Courier-Mail* and *Sunday Mail* since 1995 and have also been published by the *West Australian*. Lethbridge has won six Stanley Awards, including two Gold Stanleys (1997 and 1998).

Reg Lynch

Reg Lynch is a cartoonist, illustrator, designer and occasional curator, currently living in the north-west of Tasmania. Lynch's work regularly appears in the *Sun-Herald*. His cartoons have been published in the *Sydney Morning Herald*, *Bulletin* and the *Age*. A collection of his work, *Bulk Reg*, was published in 2000.

Alan Moir

Alan Moir has been an editorial cartoonist for the *Sydney Morning Herald* since 1984 and, prior to that, for the *Bulletin* and *Courier-Mail*. Moir was awarded a Churchill Fellowship in 1999. He has received two Walkley Awards for his work (2000 and 2006) and the United Nations Award for Political Cartooning in 1994.

Meg O'Shea

Meg O'Shea is an independent comic artist based in Sydney, on the unceded lands of the Wangal clan. In addition to self-publishing her work on online platforms and as zines, O'Shea's comics have featured in the *Nib*, the *Lily* and as part of 4A Centre for Contemporary Asian Art's digital program. They have also been collected in numerous anthologies, including *Comic Sans*; *The Threads That Connect Us*; and *Drawing Power: Women's Stories of Sexual Violence, Harassment and Survival*, which in 2020 won the Eisner Award for Best Anthology.

Jim Pavlidis

Jim Pavlidis has been at the *Age* as a press artist, designer and illustrator/cartoonist in two stints since 1987. His gap years of 1995–98 were spent at the *Independent* and *Daily Mail* newspapers in London, and at the *Paris Free Voice*. He won a Melbourne Press Club Quill Award for best artwork in 2015 and for best cartoon in 2019.

Elyce Phillips

Elyce Phillips is an illustrator, writer and comedian. Her work has appeared in *McSweeney's* and *Junkee*, and she has performed at the Melbourne International Comedy Festival, Melbourne Fringe Festival, Darwin Fringe Festival, Fringe at the Edge of the World and she appears regularly at The Improv Conspiracy in Melbourne. Her work can be found in *Heaps Comics* and on Twitter.

David Pope

David Pope grew up in Canberra and began drawing cartoons for the underground press in the 1980s. He became editorial cartoonist for the Sydney *Sun-Herald*, returning to Canberra as editorial cartoonist for the *Canberra Times* in 2008. Pope has received 12 Stanley Awards, including three Gold Stanleys for Cartoonist of the Year (2010, 2012 and 2015). He was MoAD's Political Cartoonist of the Year in 2012.

David Rowe

David Rowe is a Sydney-based cartoonist and caricaturist whose works appeared in the *Canberra Times*, the *Independent* (London), and the *Times Literary Supplement* before he joined the *Australian Financial Review* as editorial cartoonist 28 years ago. He has three Walkley and 15 Stanley awards to his credit and was MoAD's Political Cartoonist of the Year in 2013 and 2017.

Van T Rudd

Also known as Van Nishing, Queensland-born and Melbourne-based Van T Rudd is a political street artist, muralist and sculptor, who has been producing visual art for 30 years. He has long been fascinated by different methods of creating social and political commentary. He currently produces work for streets, fences and laneways in order to reach wider audiences.

John Shakespeare

John Shakespeare is a Sydney-based cartoonist, caricaturist and illustrator for the *Sydney Morning Herald*, having previously worked for the *Courier-Mail* and Sydney's *Sun*. He grew up in Brisbane, inspired by cartoonists of *MAD* and *Cracked* magazines. In 1992 Shakespeare won a Stanley Award for his caricatures.

Greg Smith

Greg 'Smithy' Smith is an editorial and sporting cartoonist based in Western Australia, where he was born. He started cartooning for the *Daily News* and, for more than a decade, has drawn cartoons for Perth's *Sunday Times* and *Perth Now*.

Phil Somerville

Freelance cartoonist Phil Somerville lives in the Blue Mountains, New South Wales. He started cartooning in the 1980s and his works have appeared in a wide range of publications including the *Sydney Morning Herald*, the *Australian*, the *Bulletin*, *Freewheeling*, *Nexus*, *Matilda*, the *Independent*, *Good Weekend Magazine* and *Limelight*. Somerville now also produces an online topical cartoon, *Line of Thought*.

John Spooner

Melbourne-based John Spooner began cartooning in the early 1970s and his works have appeared in many Australian and international publications, including the *Age* from 1977 to 2016. His cartoons now appear regularly in the *Australian*. Spooner has won many awards, including four Walkley and five Stanley awards.

Andrew Weldon

Andrew Weldon is a freelance cartoonist based in Melbourne. His cartoons appear regularly in the *Big Issue Australia*, the *Age* and the *Sydney Morning Herald*. His work has been published widely, including in the *New Yorker*, *Private Eye* and the *Spectator* (UK). Weldon has also published several books of his cartoons and illustrated children's books.

Cathy Wilcox

Sydney-based cartoonist and illustrator Cathy Wilcox has been drawing cartoons since 1989. Her work appears almost daily in the *Sydney Morning Herald* and Melbourne's *Age*. She is also an award-winning illustrator of children's books. Wilcox has received Stanley Awards for her cartoons in 1994, 1997, 2014 and 2015 and she was MoAD's Political Cartoonist of the Year in 2009, 2016 and 2020.

Published 2021 by the Museum of Australian
Democracy at Old Parliament House
PO Box 3934, Manuka ACT 2603
Phone: 02 6270 8222
Email: info@moadoph.gov.au
Website: moadoph.gov.au

ISBN: 978 0 646 84265 3
ISSN: 1835 3452

Exhibition curator: Holly Williams
Writer: Holly Williams
Researchers: Fiona Katauskas, Meg O'Shea
Introduction: Daryl Karp
Essay: Lucien Leon
Interviews: Glen Le Lievre, Karen Middleton
Illustrations: Glen Le Lievre
Designer: Claire Orrell
Publisher's editor: Thérèse Osborne

Behind the Lines is a travelling exhibition
developed at the Museum of Australian
Democracy at Old Parliament House,
proudly supported by the National
Collecting Institutions Touring and Outreach
Program, an Australian Government
program aiming to improve access to the
national collections for all Australians.

For more information about the *Behind
the Lines* exhibition: moadoph.gov.au/BTL

Front cover:
Glen Le Lievre
Choice of Viewing
animated projection
1 November 2021